Contents

Introduction

1. Syrian hamster

Syrian hamsters or *(latin: Mesocricetus auratus)* is a member of the rodent family and has been a popular little furry friend for almost 70 years.

Their popularity has stemmed from their availability and ease of keep. They take up little room and are inexpensive to purchase and to care for. Young and old alike find their cute cheeky faces and charm irresistible to ignore and a joy to own.

These little pets are available in a vast variety of coat textures and colors. The most popular of which is the *Golden* hamster, bearing a close resemblance to the original wild variety. Other coat markings are: *Tortoise shell, self colors, banded* and *dominant spotted (p4)*. Coat textures vary from smooth coated, silky coat and the ever popular *Angora* or *'Teddy bear'* hamster as it is better known. The Angora sports long hair and needs regular grooming and has different bedding requirements than the shorter haired variety.

The Syrian hamster will make for a perfect first pet for slightly older children as they can become startled, and can give an over excited young finger a nip. However, hamsters by nature are gentle and friendly little creatures and with regular handling become very tame and will even actively seek out their owners attention. As with their wild counterparts *(which are very rare and a lot smaller than pet hamsters)* the domesticated hamster still retains their nocturnal behaviors and will sleep for most of the day, coming to life and looking to play around early evening.

"Did you know I can run up to 7 miles a night"

Unlike a lot of our pet animals the Syrian hamster is a purely solitary animal and will not take to cage mates, even of the opposite sex. It is strongly advised that only one be kept at any time, as even the scent of another hamster in the same room can cause a great deal of anxiety and stress to your little pet.

Hamsters are all round great pets, and given the correct treatment *(as outlined in this book)* they will genuinely thrive in a loving environment and be a great addition to the family.

2. Origins & habitat

All Syrian hamsters that we find in the pet shops today are descendants of one female found by Dr. Israel Aharoni in 1930.

She was discovered hiding in a deep borrow with 12 young pups in the Aleppo region of Syria, *(hence the name Syrian hamster)*. However, earlier documentation has been found to suggest that the humble hamster was first documented by George Waterhouse in 1839, but wasn't studied for almost another hundred years later. In fact it wasn't until 1945 that these charming and solitary creatures began to be kept as pets. It was also around this time that the first *Hamster Fanciers Association* began.

In the wild, hamsters live lone secretive lives, in borrows dug out of the dusty earth around fields and bases of lightly grassed mounds. Syrian hamsters are extremely territorial and will only actively seek out their own kind to mate. This act in itself is very dangerous for the male hamster because if the female is not interested in the males advances she may attack him, sometimes with fatal consequences. A Syrian hamster will only tolerate others through the early weeks of their lives while weaning. Around the age of 10 to 12 weeks when either testosterone or estrogen *(dependant on sex)* begins to take hold they will no longer bear each other and will begin to fight for dominance of what they see as their territory.

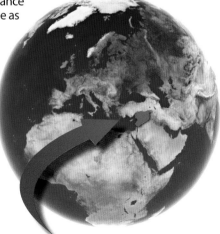

SYRIA

Top tips

Young hamster

It is best to buy your new pet at an early age, although they should be at least 6 weeks old *(see 'Life span' below)*.

You will be able to enjoy you hamster for longer and if a hamster is handled lovingly from an youth they will certainly be more friendly and relaxed around you and other humans.

3. Life span

Syrian Hamsters have an average lifespan of around 2 to 3 years of age.

Age is not a hugely important factor when purchasing or adopting your pet, however, they must be of at least 6 to 8 weeks of age to ensure that they have been weaned fully and are eating well *(see Top tip above)*.

Perfect pet?

4. Great pets

Your hamster will greatly enjoy exploring their environments. They are generally happy, inquisitive & lively little pets during early evening. This is one of the reasons why the hamster is one of the most popular pets through out the world.

Hamsters make especially good pets for those at work or school during the day. They are less active during this period, and provided they are given sufficiently quiet housing *(out of direct sunlight)*, They will sleep throughout the day, only waking to have the occasional snack from their food store or drink from their water bottle *(p11)*.

Hamsters are fun to handle, but they should only be held for short periods at a time. They can quickly become anxious and will want to seek refuge in their cage again. A tame hamster will eagerly take a healthy treat from their human friends fingers and quickly pouch this tasty morsel to be enjoyed later.

Many people enjoy watching their hamster explore the house by placing them into a hamster ball *(p12)*, this is a great way for your hamster to stretch their legs and satisfy their natural curiousity of their environments. However, be careful of any other animals around and also make sure the lid is on securely as a hamster will quickly escape if this falls off!

5. Why only one?

As mentioned before, Syrian hamsters are solitary animals and do not need the company of their own kind. Therefore, you must provide a naturally stimulating environment for you hamster *(covered later in this book)*.

In the wild, Syrian hamsters prize their borrows greatly, as they are both hard work for them to produce as well as being their precious food stores. Any imposter is feverously challenged and the borrow will be defended from intruders, sometimes with fatal force. This instinct is not lost in the pet hamster. The home you provide for them is their territory, it contains food, shelter and is their sanctuary from the outside world.

Top tips

Hamster pouches

Hamster pouches are so large and flexible that they can squeeze roughly half of their body size worth of food and treats into them!

✔

Hamster world records

Oldest hamster world record :
7 years

Longest hamster *(Syrian)*:
up to 13.5 inches (34 cm)

Hamster high jump world record:
7.8 inches (20 cm) Sweden 16 Mar '03.

Fun fact

The name *'hamster'* comes from the german word *'hamstern'* meaning *'to horde'*

Varieties

6. Popular breeds

The Syrian hamster has been successfully breed by skilled breeders for many years and now there are more than twenty-six different colors, markings and breeds, including the *dwarf hamsters*.

Below are a few of the most popular breeds:-

→→ Golden

This is the most common type of hamster coat, characterised by a dark tan color accented by dark lines running under the eyes and along the side of the face.

→→ Self colored

The *self* hamster comes in several colors and coats. Self's are hamsters with a continuous unbroken coloration. Colors most common are; chocolate, pink eye *(not to be confused with albino)* and black eye white, cream, cinnamon, black, red, tan and grey.

→→ Albino

Self whites are often confused with *albino*. While you will find albino hamsters, there is a subtle difference between it and the self whites. The albino breed is caused by a recessive gene. It is classed as recessive because it takes two genes to create the albino trait, one from each parent. You will notice with albinos that not only is the skin white, but so are the ears, feet and under the coat. With self whites, the skin still retains the natural pink pigment of a normal hamster.

→→ Dominant spotted

The *dominant spotted* is quite common amongst hamsters and is typically found in many color variations. The main body of the coat has white mottling, the underbelly, face mask, ankles and feet are normally white too.

→→ Tortoise shell

The tortoise shell is a fairly rare coated hamster to find. Typically the coat has even bands of red and black, though grey and black are also found.

→→ Satin

The satin coat is available in any color combination. The satin coat is created by having larger air pockets within the hair strands and this gives the hair the impression of luster and shine. However, two silks should never be mated together because the gene that forms the hair will be faulty, resulting in hairless hamsters.

→→ Banded

The *banded* hamster coat can be in any color or coat texture, the coat will have an even band of white running around the midsection of the body.

→→ Long haired

Long haired hamsters are often called *'Teddy bear'* hamsters, though their correct name would be *'angora'*. These breeds, as previously mentioned require special grooming and bedding. The hair forms a skirt around the rump as around the midsection. With these breeds daily grooming is required *(p14)* to prevent the hair from becoming matted and uncomfortable for your pet. The best bedding to keep these hamsters on is a paper based animal substrate as shavings will become entwined into the soft hair and may result in sores, especially between the hind legs.

Your hamster

7. Male or female?

Female hamsters are called *'does'* and male hamsters are called *'bucks'.*

It can be quite difficult to tell the sex of young *'pup'* hamsters. If you have any doubts, the store staff can confirm your hamsters' sex for you *(the two pictures and instructions below should help when you are sexing your hamster).*

Male *(Bucks)*   Female *(Does)*

The left shows the buck *(male)* while the right shows the doe *(female)*. Notice that on the buck, the space between the penis and anus is further apart than the urethra and anus of the female, notice also the small hole close to the urethra, this is the hamsters vagina. Once the males reach a level of sexual maturity, around 4 to 6 weeks the testicles descend, giving the male hamster their typical almond shaped rump, as opposed to the females rounded rump.

Ears

Bright eyes

Tail

Feet

Whiskers

Nose

8. Choosing your hamster

Ensure that the pet you choose is active and interested in its surroundings has a clean well groomed coat, clean ears, bright eyes, and a well formed body free of scabs, lumps, bald patches and signs of wounds. *Below are a few things to consider when choosing your new hamster :-*

→ Mouth

Your hamster should show no signs of dribbling or scabbing at the corners of the mouth, as this could be a sign of infection through fighting, poor health, or teeth problems.

→ Eyes

Should be bright and alert with no sign of discharge or cloudiness. If they look dull it could be sign of a more serious health issue, check regularly for foreign bodies.

→ Ears

A hamsters hearing is much better than ours. Their ears are nearly hairless, and held upright and alert. When first woken, a hamsters' ears are folded and flat, so allow time for them to extend their ears before handling *(p18)*. A small amount of wax inside the ear is perfectly normal, but if more than this is present it should be cleaned out.

→ Teeth

As with all rodents, a hamsters teeth constantly grow as they are what are called *'open rooted.'* In total, there are 16 teeth, 2 upper incisors, 2 lower incisors and 3 molars on each jaw, upper and lower quadrant. The teeth of a hamster should have a yellow tinge to them *(this denotes health)*. If the hamsters' teeth are bright white, there could be an underlying health issue *(p16)*, or poor diet.

→ Tail

The tail of a Syrian hamster is quite short, though it should during normal movement stick straight out and shows no signs of breaking or discharge around the base.

→ Paws

Hamsters paws are hairless, with front paws having four toes, and back paws having five. Ensure that the individual toes are straight, supple and the nails do not under tuck or just to the side.

→ Hiding

A hamster when first woken will most likely want to know what is going on and may be a little grumpy, allow them to wake up fully. Once awake however, they may run to seek refuge in their bolt hole, this is normal behavior and signifies that there are fit and healthy. Hamsters are what is termed *'hunted animals'* this is a natural response to a possible predator.

→ Hair

If the hair around the hamsters rump is matted, it could mean the hamster is suffering from diarrhoea *(p16)* or *'wet tail'* as it is most commonly called with hamsters. The coat should have a glossy coat with no bald patches and obviously well kept by the hamster.

→ Attitude/ personality

A hamster once awakened should show a normal inquisitive posture *(not hunched or curled)*, have a healthy appetite and sharp, lively reactions *(a lethargic hamster is one may be unhealthy)*.

→ Nose

Make sure the nose is clean, there shouldn't be any mucus in or around the nose.

Housing your hamster

9. Cages

By far the most popular type of habitat for Syrian hamsters is a cage of some description.

There are a few things to be considered when purchasing your new pets home, one of which is size. Hamsters are very active little animals and therefore require stimulation and space to play. If a cage is too small for your pets they may become bored and antisocial, leading to unpleasant behavior traits, such as biting and bar gnawing. A bored hamster may also start to over groom and chew at their own fur until they begin to strip themselves bald, in severe cases even causing open wounds.

The cage you choose must not be too high either, as hamsters enjoy nothing more than showing off their acrobatic skills by climbing their cage bars. If the cage is to tall your pet may hurt themselves when falling from the very top.

Ideally their cage should have more width and length than height *(like the one pictured)* and large enough to house the many toys and hiding places your hamster will enjoy.

Another benefit of a cage is that it is relatively easy to clean and offers your hamster better all round ventilation, as well as being a play thing in itself.

10. Vivarium/ plastic cages

Some hamster keepers keep their little pet in a *vivarium* or old fish tank *(pictured below)*.

Using these for your hamsters is fine as long as you can provide enough stimuli to the tank including hidey holes *(see Top tip p9)* and climbing toys. The downsides are that it has little ventilation, it can also be harder to clean out and your hamster may also chew at the silicon that binds the edges together. Finding a place to hang water bottles can also be an issue.

Another option is a plastic cage. These often come in a variety of colors designed to appeal to the young hamster keeper and often look best in a child's bedroom. As with the metal cages, size is important, and more floor space the better.

11. Introducing the cage

Ideally your new pets home should be already set up before purchasing your hamster.

Ask the assistant to place some of their existing bedding into the travel box with your hamster. This will not only make your pet more comfortable in the box on the way home, but will also help to relax your hamster once it is in their new home, as their scent is already present upon introduction. You should never forcibly remove the hamster from their travel box, but open it and leave it in the cage, allowing your hamster to come and explore their new environment on their own.

Let them roam freely to begin with, to explore their new surroundings. Try not to pick your new pet up for a few days in order to let them become accustomed to their new home and your presence. Speak softly to your hamster and use their name frequently.

Once they are used to their new home, be careful to acclimatize them to human contact slowly. Start by stroking your hamster with one finger while they are roaming. Next, rub a little of their shavings in your hands *(to scent your hands)*, then place a treat onto your palm, allowing your hamster to wander onto your hand to retrieve it. Do not rush this stage and if your hamster does not want to be picked up yet, respect this and allow them to wander off again to store this new treat *(see 'Handling your hamster' p18)*.

(see 'Handling your hamster' p18)

Top tips

Hidey holes

Hamsters love small spaces to squeeze through and relax in, toilet tubes, plastic cube mazes and hamster houses are all enjoyed greatly as this type of hiding place gives the same feeling of security that they would have in their wild habitats.

All hamsters must have a hiding space in their cage *(this helps to satisfy their instinct to flee when they feel threatened)*, either a wooden hidey hole *(pictured below)* or hamster house made of grass or plastic will provide enough of a snug environment to make them feel safe.

Did you know?

One human year is equal to twenty five hamster years!! That means they have a birthday about every two weeks.

3.

1. Hamster suitable cage.
2. A converted aquarium tank.
3. Small pet wooden hidey hole & hamster (banded syrian).

The hamsters food guide

12. Food glorious food

All animals, like humans, have different tastes and what one hamster loves, another will simply sniff at and ignore.

So get to know what your hamster really enjoys, and use this as a treat when you place them back into their cage to re-enforce that they have been good when appropriate.

There are many food types to choose from, though you should never change foods to quickly from one brand to another as this can cause stomach upsets.

The most common staple diet for hamsters is in the form of muesli that contains all of the nutrients needed to keep your hamster healthy and happy. **Hamster muesli** *(pictured below)* is a complete food and contains all of the vitamins and proteins they need, this includes meat proteins such as chicken. This is because hamsters are omnivores and they would eat small grubs and insects in the wild, as well as seeds and roots.

13. Good treat foods

Good treat foods for hamsters include:

Apple, banana, blackberries, blueberries, grapes, mango, melon, carrot, broccoli, unsalted peanuts, monkey nuts.

These foods must only be given as an occasional treat and in very small portions, remember, your hamster has only a small stomach and will quickly become poorly if too much is given.

Bad foods:

Almonds (contains cyanic acid), apple seeds, human chocolate, pork products, potatoes, kidney beans, grape seeds, avocado (contains cardiac glycosides), raw rhubarb, tomato leaves, oranges or tangerines (citrus fruits are to acid for their digestive system), watermelon (the water content causes diarrhoea), peach stone & leaves, garlic, onions, chives.

1.

Syrian hamster; Cinnamon Satin.

2.

3.

14. Treats

Treats specifically designed for your hamster are readily available through your local pet shop.

These include **hanging stick treats**, often made with **nuts** and **seeds**, **animal chocolate drops** *(pictured above)* as well as **honey drops**. **Natural wood treat packs** are greatly received and enjoyed to the fullest, as they mimic the food they would forage for in the wild.

Hamsters also enjoy the occasional piece of **cooked chicken** or **beef**. But only in small amounts as this may cause diarrhoea and obesity if given to often and in too large a quantity.

15. Pellets

These are specially made from either a pellet *(sometimes referred to as laboratory blocks)* or a biscuit.

The benefits of feeding pellet or biscuit food is that it not only helps keep your hamsters teeth in good condition and well worn, it also stops your pet from **selective feeding** *(when your hamster only eats the parts of the food that they want, often leaving the parts of food in the muesli that are of real benefit to them)*.

4.

Important!

Hamsters are naturally drawn to water so if your pet escapes, try placing a small bowl of water inside a bucket. Place a ladder up to the top and bedding in the bottom to try to catch them.

16. Water

The amount of water your hamster needs will vary, so it is always advisable that you have a constant supply of water within easy reach of your pet.

The water should be available in a bottle as a bowl will quickly become soiled and unhealthy for you pet to drink. A good idea is to mark the fill level of their water bottle and refresh daily. This enables you to not only see how much your pet drinks, but also if there are any changes in the quantity consumed.

1. Hamster muesli.
2. Hamster chocolate drops.
3. Hamster friendly wood mix.
4. Water bottle.

Play time

17. Exercise

Hamsters are lively and energetic little animals and require a great deal of exercise to keep them in good condition and help them live a long and fit life.

In the wild, a hamster will run around up to 8 km (5 miles) a night in the search for food and water. This need to run is a compulsion your pet hamster still has. Without the opportunity to express this natural instinct your hamster may become very lazy, sleep a lot more and will become overweight and as a result, as with humans, hamsters can experience similar health problems that arise as a result of being overweight.

If your pet does get overweight it will have higher tendencies for heart disease, diabetes, bladder infections, respiratory problems and joint conditions. A large cage with enough room to play and a hamster wheel can help keep your pet in good shape and ensure that they live a rich and healthy life.

Another great way to keep your hamster in good health is to place them into a hamster ball *(pictured below, left)*, not only will this be great fun to watch, but a great way for your hamster to work off extra energy they have, as well as giving their little muscles a work out.

1.

18. Play

In their natural environment hamsters only play when they are young pups.

In this play period they learn how to fight and to hunt. When they reach adulthood they have no need to play as such, and certainly will not play with other hamsters. They do however love to explore, work out puzzles, run and greatly enjoy the affections of their human friends.

2.

Runner ball

Balls are great fun for your hamster. A hamster ball will be great, but you must ensure that you supervise them during their exercise as they may escape.

19. Accessories

Different hamsters enjoy different types of toys but all enjoy the simple pleasure of running through cardboard mazes in the search for a tasty hidden treat. Cardboard tubes, small cardboard boxes and a wheel are ideal for all hamsters as are gnaw blocks *(p15)* and toys they can drag around.

The best way to find your pets favorite is to simply experiment until you find a toy that entertains your particular pet. Usually the simpler the toy the better.

Some of the guinea pig favorites are:
A toilet paper tube | a medium sized cardboard box | willow balls | plastic animal ball with bell | hanging fruit wood toys | a straw basket | tubes | plastic extensions for cages | maze.

Change the toys, houses, and locations frequently to keep things fresh and interesting for your pet.

Keep toys, houses and food dishes away from the walls and corners of the cage. Not only will they use a certain corner of the cage as their toilet but you will need to keep the walls of the cage clear to allow them room to exercise *(they will use this space to run around the perimeter and to climb)*.

1. Runner ball.
2. Plastic extension tubes.
3. Wooden log hidey hole.
4. Sand bath *(chinchilla sand)*.
5. Exercise wheel & hamster *(Syrian; cinnamon teddy)*.

4.

5.

3.

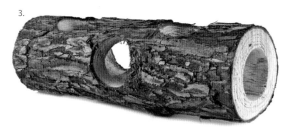

NB. Not all hamsters like exercise wheels, so don't be worried if they don't want to use it. Just make sure they have a way to exercise.

Hamster grooming

20. Grooming

Grooming should be part of your daily play routine when handling your hamster

This activity will not only prove to be of great enjoyment for your hamster but will also gives you an opportunity to perform a health check on your pet. Regular contact of this nature will offer you a greater insight into any changes in your hamsters body and coat conditions which can help you in recognising signs of illness *(if you are unsure of anything that you may find, you should consult your veterinary as soon as possible)*.

Hamsters are very clean and tidy little animals and spend a great deal of their time grooming themselves and cleaning their coats. They don't tend to molt in the traditional sense as guinea pigs or rabbits do because their coat does not need changing as often.

It is important that the rough/ long haired varieties of hamster are brushed regularly and their hair is kept in a good condition. Their hair is prone to becoming matted and knotted and this can become quite unpleasant and painful for your hamster if left unchecked. It is best to groom long haired breeds daily to prevent this.

To groom your hamster you will need a:
Brush: a soft bristle tooth brush is best
Nail trimmer: guillotine type or human kind can work as well.

21. Trimming nails

We recommend you take your hamster to a vet or an experienced hamster keeper for nail trimming.

However, in time and with the relative experience you may find that you can do it yourself. It is still advised that you first speak to a veterinary surgeon who can guide you through the technique of nail trimming.

On the whole, hamsters do tend to their own nails and the climbing and scratching they do while creating their little borrows in the shaving keeps them in good condition. However, as your hamster ages, its nails will grow faster than they will wear down so you will inevitably have to do this for them at some point.

1.

It is important to note that there is part within the nail called the *'quick,'* this vein is where the blood vessels and nerve endings are located. If you do accidently cut into the *quick* you will cause bleeding as well as considerable pain to your pet. The aim is just to clip the sharp tip of the nail without damaging the *quick.*

1. Hamster friendly nail trimmer.

Health

22. Good health

To ensure your hamster remains in good health, make sure that their diet has an adequate intake of vitamins and minerals, through a balanced, complete, high quality diet.

23. Wood gnaws

Wood gnaws are available in pet shops or you can provide your own by supplying your hamster with a piece of unsprayed fruit branch or untreated wood block to gnaw on.

These will provide your pet with something on which to keep its teeth nice and trim. It would be a good idea to age the branches if you choose to use these, as the drying process is extremely important as some of these branches are poisonous while fresh.

24. Health checks

Here's a few easy health checks that you can do yourself when you are grooming or playing with your pet.

Check through your hamsters coat by running the tip of your finger against the lay of the hair. If there is any dry skin or bald spots, these may be indicative of a fungal or parasitic skin condition.

Check that its teeth are not broken, loose or over growing.

Checks to see if the nose is dry, eyes are bright and that the hamsters movements are quick, decisive and curious about their surroundings *(see p7)*.

Did you know?

Did you know the word *'rodent'* is derived from the Latin word *'rodere'* which means *'to gnaw'*.

Syrian hamster; Mink.

25. Health problems

→→ Constipation and diarrhoea

This should be taken very seriously, they can be caused by a bad diet, illness or stress. *Consult a vet if you have any queries.*

→→ Respiratory infections

Hamsters are prone to respiratory infections and will usually have very similar symptoms to that of the human common cold.

However, it can have a more serious impact on hamsters and should not be left untreated as it can lead to *pneumonia*. Keep out of damp, drafty environments and if symptoms continue, consult your veterinary for further advice.

Hamsters can catch a human cold or flu virus too, so it is recommended that if you are ill with one of these you should avoid handling you pet until you are better.

→→ Parasites

Scratching is a common symptom of a skin complaint often brought about by parasites like *lice, mites* and *fleas.*

Hamsters are usually free from parasites but should your pet get an infestation, treat with a specialised medicated shampoo, mild insecticide powder or small animal *Spot On* drop. If you have any queries, seek veterinary advice.

• •

If you think one of your hamster is ill, take your pet to a qualified vet.

→→ Eye injuries

These are fairly common in hamsters. Usually caused by sharp objects or shavings flying into the eye while digging, exploring or falling whilst climbing.

A saline wash flush the eye of any foreign bodies but consult your vet if problems persist.

Cage care

26. Home sweet home

A covering is required for your hamsters cage floor, to provide a comfortable surface for it to rest on, as well as absorbing urine.

The most common type of floor covering available is wood shavings. Fine sawdust should be avoided as this can cause irritation to the eyes and to the lungs. Cedar shavings *(usually distinguished by a red tint)* should not be used as the *phenols* they contain can cause severe irritations in small animals. **Pine wood shavings** cause less problems than cedar and **kiln dried pine** can also be used without problems.

You should steer clear of any scented shavings as these can cause irritation to your hamster and can cause distress by masking their scent. Corn cob bedding is not recommended either, it tends to grow mould, and this can be eaten by or get trapped in their pouches and swell.

Wood shavings from hardwoods such as aspen or small animal litter made from wood pulp are the safest forms of floor covering to use.

27. Cage cleaning

It has been said that hamsters are relatively odourless pets, which is true to a degree. However, even an odourless pets cage will start to smell if it is not cleaned for an extended period.

Urine soaked bedding, feces and decaying vegetable matter all make your pets cage an unpleasant place to live as well as encouraging flies and other undesirable pests to take hold.

→ Remove your hamster and make sure you place them in a safe and secure place before you begin cleaning. A plastic small animal carrier or tank is suitable.

→ Once a day you should remove all droppings and any uneaten fresh food. Ideally any fresh food given as a treat should be fed the night before your weekly clean.

→ Check that the bedding and cage litter is dry *(as damp conditions are very bad for small animals).*

→ Tidy the sleeping area and ensure that they have fresh clean water and the bottle is free of algae *(use a mild animal safe detergent once a week to clean the water bottle, rinse thoroughly and replace with fresh water in the hutch).*

→ Once a week, clean the whole cage using a brush and good animal-friendly cleaning disinfectant *(wait until the inside of the cage and base is completely dry before replacing the litter and bedding and putting hamster back in).*

Handling your hamster

28. Gently does it

Hamsters by nature are timid animals and will often shirk their owners attention initially, but if handled gently from an early age, they will soon become accustomed to you and being picked up and held.

To begin with, remember that you are much bigger than your hamster. Try not to reach down on top of your pet as their close range sight is very poor and it may think that you are a predator. In the wild hamsters are often hunted from above by birds of prey and your hand can easily be confused for one if you approach them from above.

You should first, rub some of their bedding in your hands to place their scent on you. Then softly stroke their head and back, hamsters do not like their cheeks or faces being touched so be careful.

Speak softly to your pet, using their name frequently and reassuringly. Place a favored treat on the palm of your hand and lay it down back down flat against the cage base, and wait for you hamster to come to you. Once your hamster is comfortable retrieving the treat from your hand, you can move onto the next stage.

Once your hamster is happy coming to your hand for their treat, wait until they are settled and sniffing on your hand, gently raise hand out of the cage, cupping your free hand around them to prevent them from falling or scuttling off as they are lifted. Keep them calm throughout the lifting process.

Talk gently to your hamster whilst gently stroking their back with your thumb. After you have gained their trust and they feel safe gently pull them into your chest and gently stroke their backs talking softly to them.

If you are new to hamsters then you should kneel down on the floor to lift them up, this will minimize the chance of any injury should your hamster wriggle free. They are fragile creatures and can suffer greatly if dropped, even if from a short heights.

29. Small children and safety

Children should be sat down *(preferably on the floor)*, when you pass the hamster to them.

Be prepared to remove the hamster if it becomes agitated. A child will sometimes struggle to keep a hold of a small animal and if they squeeze their pet to tightly it may bite or worse, become injured itself through an accidental tight grasp.

Teach your children to be gentle and to only stroke the hair in the direction the hair is growing.

When placing your hamster back in their cage, they can become quite excited, so be extra careful not to drop them. Try to release your hold on them only once they are safely on the floor of your cage.

30. Stroking

If your hamster is not in the mood for stroking they will let you know by turning their heads sharply toward you and raising their front paws, or they may *'crackle'* at you.

Never stroke a hamsters stomach as this is a sign of dominance and they become quite scared or bite.

31. Vocalizations

Hamsters are not particularly vocal little animals, making only the occasional squeak on rare occasions. One sound you may hear is *'Crackling'.*

→ **Crackling**

Sounds a little like an electric discharge. This sound is used to warn off predators or to show fear. If this sound is not heeded you may receive a rather nasty nip. If your hamster makes this noise as you approach, it is best to leave them alone until they calm down.

"Did you know? I can be taught to recognise my name and come to you when called."

Syrian hamster; banded.

Know your hamster

32. Hamster anatomy

The anatomy of the hamster is the result of years of evolution and shows the adaptations it has had to undertake to survive.

Their body is designed for its main tasks, eating, reproducing and fleeing from predators.

Their heightened senses and ability to spot danger early and run for cover, gave them an evolutionary edge and is the main reason that the rodent species has flourished where others have failed.

All hamsters posses the same physical features of a flat nose, short legs and very short tail.

The average life span of a hamster is between 2 and 3 years. The average weight of an adult is approximately 6.2 oz (182 g) and they thrive at an ambient temperature of 100°F (38°C).

If they become to cold your hamster may hibernate, if this does happen, gently place them onto a warm towel and put them into a warm room or airing cupboard to bring them back around. Do not try to wake them, allow them time come around in their own time.

Syrian hamster; Golden.

33. Know your hamsters behavior

→ **Jumping**

Jumping straight up in the air is a typical display of joy.

→ **Sitting up**

Sitting up with their teeth bared in what looks like a smile with their paws held in front typically means back away I am about to bite.

→ **Rolling on to their backs**

Fear, submissive, offering of peace.

→ **Mouth wide open, showing teeth and crackling**

Vocal warning to predators.

→ **Stretching the head forwards and walking in jerks**

Watchful and alert.

→ **Retracting legs under body and backed up against a wall**

Helpless, scared and needing protection.

→ **Stress**

This will impact on your pets immune system and can adversely affect its ability to fight off infections.

Keep your hamster away from extreme temperatures and drafts, as well as intimidating animals/ people. To relieve stress make sure your hamster has plenty of places in which to retreat if they feel threatened *(Top tips p9).*

Breeding advice

34. Golden rules of breeding

Before even considering breeding hamsters, it is best to make sure that you can find homes for the inevitable litter.

The average litter of pups is between 4 to 8, although it is not strange for there to be as many as 12 in a litter.

You must never interfere with the mother when she has had her litter. She will see this interaction between you and her young as a threat and she may eat her pups. This is a response still held from the wild, where she will eat the pups to gain the energy she needs to run for a great distance to find a new home and escape the perceived danger.

After she has become pregnant you will find that her personality may change from being cute and gentle, seeking you're attention, to being guarded and aggressive. She becomes like this as she wants to be left alone to build her nest and raise her young. Do not try to hold her during this stage as she may bite or miscarry because of the stress. Just before she has her pups and while she is nursing them it is of vital importance that you do not try to clean out her nest area, she will do this for you by throwing out any soiled bedding. Simply remove this and place fresh into the cage for her to take back into her nesting place.

The whole gestation and weaning period takes no longer than 45 days, but throughout this time the mother will need extra food, extra bedding and the addition of a *mineral stone* to her cage as well as extra vitamins in her water will be greatly appreciated.

35. Preparing the cage

Provide the mother with extra bedding and at least 2 houses or nesting areas in which to raise her pups.

A single layered cage is better as even though her pups are born blind, they do still tend to wander around after about 4 days and can easily become lost and disorientated. Make sure that the water bottle is at a reachable height for the young arrivals and that food is easily accessible to them for when they begin to eat solids. It is a good idea to have enough space outside of the nesting area for the mother to throw out soiled bedding for you to collect and fresh to be placed, with as little interaction as possible from yourself.

36. Introductions

The introduction of a Syrian male to a female is not to be taken lightly and you may find that you will need more than one male to successfully find a suitor for her.

Females are quite discerning when it comes to mating and the whole process should be done no later than 4 months, while she is at her prime. The male should be around 3 months old for a better chance of successful acceptance and mating. The male must always be introduced to the female in a neutral territory or just after she has been cleaned out as in the wild the female will spring clean her borrow when it is time to mate and the male will seek her out. A female introduced to a male will be regarded as inferior and a threat to his territory and attacked.

The display and mating process should only be allowed to go on for 10 minutes, after which remove the male, even if he has not mounted the female. If she has not raised her rump *(called 'displaying')* to the male after he has shown an interest during this time she will attack him. If this is the case, wait until the next day and try again. If still she shows no sign of interest then maybe he is not her choice so try another male. You should never leave the two hamsters alone while this is going on as you will not be able to intervene should she reject him. Once she has displayed and the male mounts her, this lasts only around 30 seconds and he retreats away, remove him straight away otherwise she will attack him as she no longer needs him and must get on with her nest building in preparation.

Titles in series

 **The Kitten**
Top tips for a happy healthy pet

 **The Goldfish**
Top tips for a happy healthy pet

 **The Rabbit**
Top tips for a happy healthy pet

 **The Hamster**
Top tips for a happy healthy pet

 **The Gerbil**
Top tips for a happy healthy pet

 **Dwarf Rabbit**
Top tips for a happy healthy pet

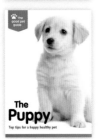 **The Puppy**
Top tips for a happy healthy pet

 **The Guinea Pig**
Top tips for a happy healthy pet

 **Dwarf Hamster**
Top tips for a happy healthy pet

 **The Degu**
Top tips for a happy healthy pet

magnet® steel &
publishing limited

Magnet & Steel Publishing Ltd
Unit 6
Vale Business Park,
Llandow, United Kingdom. CF71 7PF
sales@magnetandsteelpublishing.com